Copyright © 2025 Kieran and Breann Mabey
Print: 979-8-218-57690-5 (hardcover)
First Edition
Illustrations by: William Bradford

All rights reserved. No part of this publication may be reproduced, distributed, or transmitted in any form or by any means, including photocopying, recording, or other electronic or mechanical methods, without the prior written permission of the publisher, except in the case of brief quotations embodied in critical reviews and certain other noncommercial uses permitted by copyright law. For permission requests, contact Lange Leadership Coaching, LLC - **Mabey Made** | kcbremabey@gmail.com | kieranmabey.com | @mabey_made

Printed in the United States of America & Canada

Welcome to the enchanting journey of baby naming! Naming your child is a momentous and magical affair—let us lend a helping hand. Inside these pages you'll find stepping stones of inspiration, tradition, and love for each stride of this journey.

Before delving in, take a moment to personalize this book with your own touch of affection. Whether you're gifting this book as a joyful friend, as a proud grandparent, or as expecting parents yourselves, here's a space awaiting your heartfelt words. So use this page to pen a special note, a wish for the baby's bright future, or a reflection on the joys of parenthood. Let your note become a treasured keepsake, adding warmth and meaning to these first steps of all that is in a name.

This small book does claim
to set your mind aflame,
so you can then proclaim
that which even Shakespeare asked in vain:

WHAT'S IN A NAME?

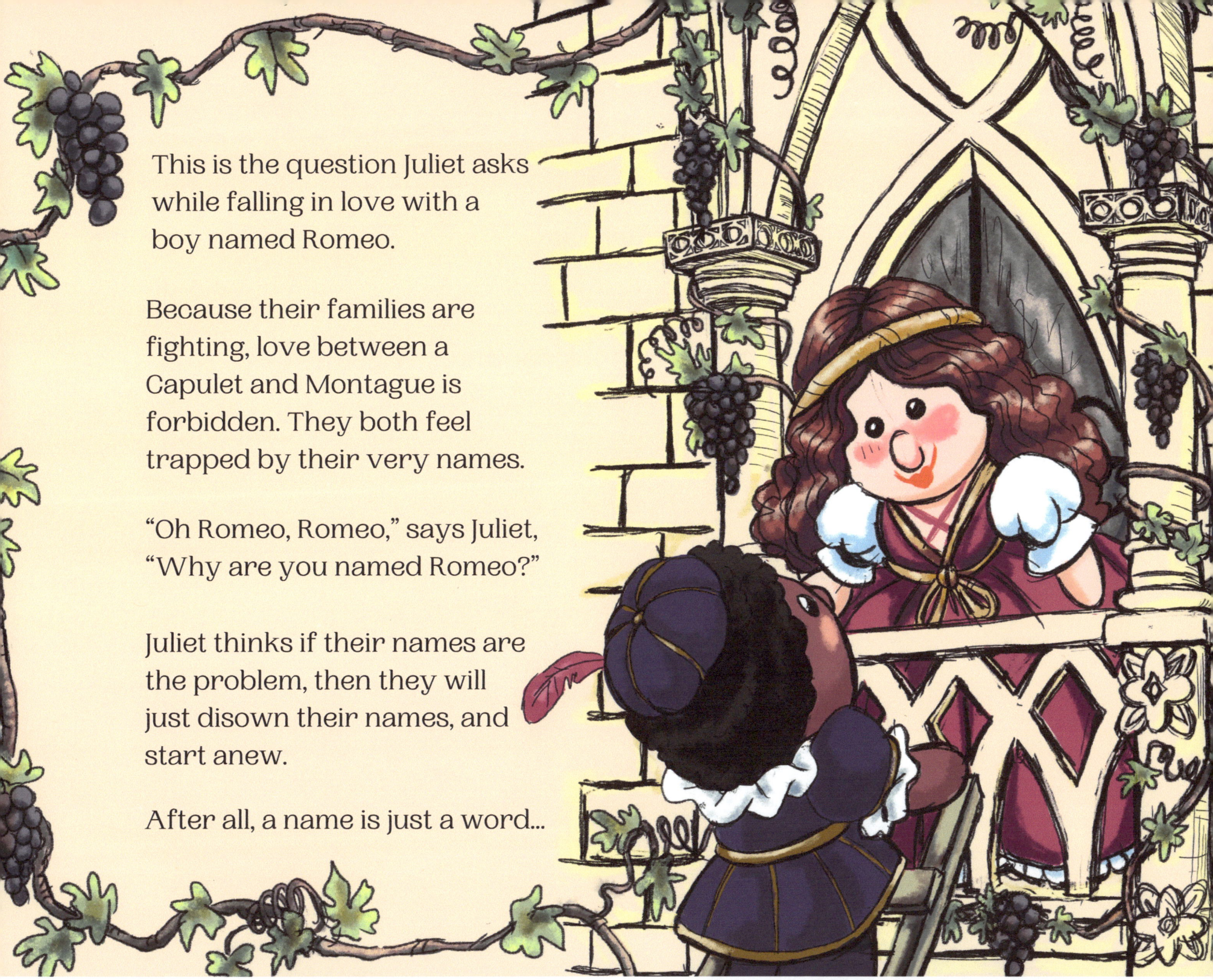

This is the question Juliet asks while falling in love with a boy named Romeo.

Because their families are fighting, love between a Capulet and Montague is forbidden. They both feel trapped by their very names.

"Oh Romeo, Romeo," says Juliet, "Why are you named Romeo?"

Juliet thinks if their names are the problem, then they will just disown their names, and start anew.

After all, a name is just a word...

Alas, a name is not just a word.

As Shakespeare knew, a name might tell you about a person's history and culture, their language and class, or their race and religion.

So, what's in a name?

A name holds heaps: hiding inside and hunching behind, or hanging above and hinting ahead.

But this is a little book for such a big question.

So let's shrink things smaller. In other words, let's make this *baby-sized*.

After all, every baby born into the world is given a name…

THIS IS THE STORY OF YOUR NAME.

THIS IS THE STORY OF WHY WE NAMED YOU:

_____

There's no shortage of names in the world, and for every name there may be many reasons as to why it was chosen. So we took all the possible reasons for choosing any name, and we put them into just six categories.

Now, with each turn of the page,
you'll learn one more part of what's held in your name.

Along the way, we'll share other names we considered—
all the close calls you were almost called.

You may not be the only person with your name,
but your name is the only one with this story.

LEGACY

A birth is a new beginning, bringing hope for what's in store,
but every new beginning always belongs to a before.
So when we thought of your name, we looked back through family lore.

Names from members past, forever still held dear.
When we pass their names on, it's like a part of them stays here.

Linking past and present, in a loving blend,
your name part of a story—one without an end.

CENTRAL CHARACTERS WE CONSIDERED FROM THE STORY OF OUR LIFE & LEGACY:

CIRCLE HOW IMPORTANT THIS FACTOR IS:

THE REASON

LOVE THIS

SO, SO

LANGUAGE, CULTURE, & MEANING

Just like babies come from parents, did you know that words get born too?
A mother tongue and fatherland, from which their meaning is imbued.

Your name may come from the same place where you find yourself today,
or sometimes your name connects you to a place that's far away.

Just like little kids, languages stretch and grow.
They might come from one place,
but then travel   to   and   fro.

But just like you, wherever they go,
they'll always carry deep inside,
that special story, all their own
from where they did reside.

THIS IS WHERE YOUR NAME COMES FROM, AND WHAT IT MEANS:

CIRCLE HOW IMPORTANT THIS FACTOR IS:

THE REASON

LOVE THIS

SO, SO

FIT: MIDDLE & SURNAME

When it comes to names, you'll find you've got more than just one,
so when we picked your first, it didn't mean that we were done.

If a name is like a story, it needs a beginning, middle, and end.
When we put them all together, we hope they each hold hands like friends.

In the beginning, when you're smallest, people only call the first.
Then, once you grow older, that will usually get reversed,
because they'll call you by your last name, while the others get submersed.

Your middle name can spend its whole life hiding, hardly ever getting called.

But sometimes it breaks free and stands tall,
and your middle name becomes
the one called most of all.

THIS IS WHAT WE THOUGHT ABOUT HOW YOUR FULL NAME FITS TOGETHER:

CIRCLE HOW IMPORTANT THIS FACTOR IS:

THE REASON

LOVE THIS

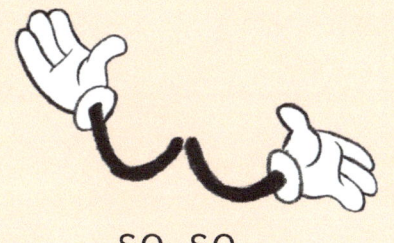

SO, SO

NICKNAMES

Just because you've got a nice name,
doesn't mean everyone will call you the same.
Twist it and tweak it, like it's all a big game,
and that's the way that you make a nickname.

Sometimes your name might get chopped right in half,
or stretched out and made longer, all for a laugh.

These special names are usually saved, just for family and friends,
but sometimes they spread,
and soon enough, everyone calls you the nickname instead!

The line between names and nicknames can become blurry in a hurry.
So when thinking of what you'll be named,
we carefully considered some nicknames contained.

NAME

WHEN IT COMES TO YOUR NAME, THESE ARE THE NICKNAMES WE SAW HIDING WITHIN:

CIRCLE HOW IMPORTANT THIS FACTOR IS:

THE REASON

LOVE THIS

SO, SO

NICKNAMES

ASSOCIATIONS

Names evoke memories and release emotions.
Take us back in time and across oceans.

Amidst such affiliations, our names flow and ebb,
single spoken threads, within tangled worded webs.

Reaching back through legend and myth and times of yore,
names pulled from pages of favourite books penned;
Reminiscing of a place or person or time from before,
names flow from far places and from closest friends.

Whether common, unique, or somewhere in between,
one they've often heard, or one they've hardly seen,
a name can have so many associations, it's bursting at the seams.

WHEN IT COMES TO THE WEBS YOUR NAME WILL SPIN, THESE ARE THE THREADS WE SAW WITHIN:

CIRCLE HOW IMPORTANT THIS FACTOR IS:

THE REASON

LOVE THIS

SO, SO

AESTHETICS

Every name always starts in the mouth and ends in the ears,
but the path that it takes can be more or less clear.

Does it take time on the tongue, with slow syllable steps?
Then when people first meet you they may need some attempts.

Or does is it leap from the lips, and fly fast from the face?
Smooth sailing, mouth to ears, it all falls into place.

A name spends a lot of its time moving through mouths and entering into ears,
so we took some time to sound out yours, before you got here.

THIS IS HOW WE FEEL WHEN WE SAY AND HEAR YOUR NAME:

CIRCLE HOW IMPORTANT THIS FACTOR IS:

THE REASON

LOVE THIS

SO, SO

THIS IS THE STORY OF YOUR NAME.

Or at least the part of it to which we can lay claim.
For the story you write, as you move through the world, may not end the same.

You might like it and love it and keep it forever.
Or as Juliet, maybe you'll one day want to swap it for one that suits better.

Whether you mold it, change it, or keep it that way,
 we'll always love you, no matter the day.

As we turn this last page,
 you have now learnt all that is held in your name.

Now the story of your name continues with you.
We hope you cherish it, as much as we do you.

THIS LITTLE BOOK IS JUST THE BEGINNING...

Tape photo here!

COMPARISON CHART

Feel free to list any names here, even the fun ones you couldn't agree on.
Maybe one day your child will look back and laugh!

Categories	PARENT *:	PARENT †:	Top Picks
	Names	Names	
Legacy			
Language, Culture, & Meaning			
Fit: Middle & Surname			
Nicknames			
Associations			
Aesthetics			

NAME NOTES

Scribble, sketch, and dream with glee—your perfect name awaits thee!

NAME NOSTALGIA LANE

YEARS FROM NOW, REVISIT THIS PAGE, FINISH YOUR NAME'S STORY, NOW YOU'VE COME OF AGE

- What do you like about your name?
- If you could change your name, would you? Why or why not?
- Do you feel connected to anyone else with the same name?
- Do you feel your name fits your personality? How so?
- Are there any nicknames you prefer over your given name?
- Does anything annoy you about your name?
- Has your opinion of your name changed over time?
- What do you think your name says about you to other people?
- What is the first thing that comes to mind when you hear your name?

For now this story has no more to say,
Then this completes the story of _____'s name.

www.ingramcontent.com/pod-product-compliance
Lightning Source LLC
Chambersburg PA
CBHW050849010526
44107CB00018BA/1226